WORLD W AUSCHWITZ

A History From Beginning to End

Copyright © 2017 by Hourly History.

All rights reserved.

Table of Contents

Introduction
In the Beginning, Prejudice
Adolf Hitler and the Preservation of the Aryan Race
The Nazis in Charge
The Final Solution to the Jewish Question
The Angel of Death
Life in Auschwitz
Liberation and Judgment

Introduction

Nations and governments have participated in genocide since wars began, but there was something different about the Nazi regime's deliberate, methodical extermination of Jews, homosexuals, Jehovah's Witnesses, Communists, the disabled, and Gypsies. Just as Holocaust has come to be the definition of a systemic process of genocide against a segment of the population, Auschwitz has come to symbolize the means by which that process took place. The largest and most efficient, if such a gruesomely mundane description can be used, of the camps, Auschwitz was a death sentence from the moment it was constructed.

Between 1933, when Adolf Hitler came to power in Germany, and 1945, when the Nazi regime fell to Allied forces, more than 3.5 million Germans spent time in concentration camps. But concentration camps were not designed for the eradication of a race; they were founded to contain opponents of the German Reich. Approximately 77,000 were executed in the concentration camps. However, the extermination camps set up by the Nazis for the deliberate murder of those ethnic, religious and political groups it regarded as inferior, had a much higher death toll and a far more macabre mission.

After the Nazi takeover of Poland, the Germans began to create camps there and in areas where large groups of Jews lived. The German concept of this evil real estate allowed them to remove German Jews from Germany and do so quickly. The crime of the detainees was identified by the triangular badges that they were forced to wear: political prisoners and Communists wore red; homosexuals were identified by the color pink; Jehovah's Witnesses wore purple; the Gypsies or Romani wore brown, and the Jews wore yellow.

During its years of operation, more than one million prisoners were killed at Auschwitz, the most notorious of the German camps. It's impossible to know the complete death toll because so many prisoners died on the way; others, who were sent to the gas chambers upon arrival, increased the death toll. In addition to the murdered Jews, more than 70,000 Poles and nearly 20,000 Gypsies and Soviet prisoners of war died at Auschwitz as well. As the camp was liberated, the remaining inmates, many of whom were seconds away from death, served as a reminder that the world could never forget what took place there.

Other populations have been murdered, massacred, and violated. Man's inhumanity to man is not unique to any particular era or country. But just as nations have their capital cities, the Holocaust has its own horrifying capital, and that capital is Auschwitz, where technology was sadistically used to kill, and science was distorted to serve the maniacal ends of a country that allowed itself to believe the promises of a madman.

Today the site is a museum where research is conducted into the Holocaust. Visitors from all over the world go to the museum to witness for themselves what the persecuted victims of Nazi genocide endured. As often as the stories are told, it is not enough. In order for the world to remember, the story of Auschwitz must be told again and again.

Chapter One

In the Beginning, Prejudice

"Then answered all the people and said, 'His blood be on us and on our children.'"

—Matthew 27:25

In a Christianized Europe, persecution of the Jews was regarded as a justified response of retaliation against the Jews. The Jews had engineered the crucifixion of Jesus Christ, and from that act, they had taken on the sin of his murder. But in the early days after the death of Christ, it was Christians who were the persecuted ones. The man destined to become the most influential evangelist of the Christian faith, Paul of Tarsus, was a devout Jew who was known and feared in the young church for the zeal with which he hunted down Christians. That was until his conversion on the road to Damascus, after which time he dedicated his life to preaching the gospel and converting others to the new faith that started as an offshoot of Judaism.

For the Gentile converts who were unfamiliar with Judaism and the close ties between the new sect and the established Jewish faith which Jesus had practiced, anti-Semitism was not unfamiliar. The Gospel of John cast aspersions on the Jewish leaders who were seen as hostile to the growth of the new faith. The Christian Church, as it grew, began to regard itself as superior to the Jews and writings reflect the belief that Jews, who had rejected Jesus, were themselves rejected. They were destined to wander the land, homeless and unwanted, for their sin against Christ.

The Roman Empire, the dominant power in the region, tolerated most faiths but drew the line at Christianity. When a fire destroyed much of Rome during the reign of Emperor Nero in 64 CE, there was renewed vigor in executing the Christians. Under Emperor Trajan, Christians were given the opportunity to recant and agree to worship the Roman gods. If they refused, they were executed. Later, antipathy to Christians moderated somewhat; Emperor Hadrian ruled that when a Christian was brought to trial, it was necessary to prove that an illegal act had been committed before the Christian could be condemned.

For three hundred years under imperial rule, Christianity continued to be viewed as an unpopular faith. Because they would not worship the many gods of the Romans, blame was placed on them when a natural disaster or catastrophe befell the community. Despite the persecution, Christianity continued to grow and to develop ecclesiastical organization as they stubbornly refused to be cowed by the authorities seeking to stamp out their faith.

In 257 CE, Emperor Valerian banished Christian bishops, shut down Christian worship sites and cemeteries, and forbade anyone to enter Christian locations. But the Christians were not subdued by the edict and continued to observe their faith, driving Valerian to order the execution of Christian clergy and confiscate church property. When Diocletian became the emperor, he was not personally opposed to the religion; in fact, there were members of his family who were followers of Jesus Christ. But he was influenced by his advisors and the persecution intensified as Christians were purged from the Roman army and the civil service. Christian worship services were forbidden and churches destroyed; holy writings were burned; Christians of high rank in the government were denied their civil rights.

The role of Christians changed dramatically upon the accession of Constantine to the imperial throne. On the night before a momentous battle, Constantine dreamed that Jesus Christ came to him and told him to use the cross as his symbol in order to conquer his enemies. With victory in battle and his dominance in Rome, Constantine's policy of endorsement shifted the balance of power. No longer were Christians the downtrodden and the persecuted. The tables had turned, but the empowered Christians did not follow the example of the Prince of Peace in their dealings with other faiths.

By the Middle Ages, Europe had been Christianized and Jews were a powerless minority, often denied citizenship. In some countries, they could not hold positions in government or join the army. In 1096, French knights who had returned from the First Crusade massacred Jews in France and Germany. Now it was the Jews who were falsely accused of grotesque acts, including the claim that, in order to make Passover bread, the Jews sacrificed Christian children and took their blood as an ingredient. In the twelfth century, Jews were required to wear a yellow badge to indicate their membership in a despised and accursed religion, a practice which would resurface in the twentieth century as the Nazis adopted ways to mark Jews. Another institution, the ghetto, had its roots in the medieval era, as Jewish communities were segregated from the Christian population.

The Jews, however despised they might have been by the Christians who held power, had an important economic role in Christian society. Christian rules forbade each other from charging interest when money was borrowed. Jews, however, were not bound by this stricture and were able to loan money. The stereotype of the rich, stingy Jewish moneylender would endure throughout the medieval ages and even beyond as resentment against Jewish financial acumen would be a frequent source of hostility toward the religion.

With the growth of commerce during the late Middle Ages, Jewish success in the financial sector became an established part of the economic foundation of the countries. It was inevitable that resentment would result from envy. In 1290, England had expelled its Jewish residents; France, Germany, Portugal, Provence, and the Papal States would do the same from the fourteenth to the sixteenth centuries. Spain offered its Jewish population the option of converting to Christianity, but even those who converted were distrusted and fell into the clutches of the Spanish Inquisition. Exiled from Western Europe where they had lived for centuries, many Jews migrated to Poland and Russia.

The many benefits that Jewish residents brought to their adoptive countries were disregarded. The Jewish role in trade was a significant one. They also played an important role in the culture of their societies. In Spain, before their expulsion, Jewish writers, philosophers, and physicians shared prominence with Christian and Muslim members of those professions.

The Protestant Reformation did not bring about a transformation in attitudes toward Jews. Martin Luther made use of Jewish scholars when he was translating Hebrew scriptures into German, but he could not forgive the Jews for their role in the death of Jesus. He wrote, "We are at fault for not slaying them. Rather we allow them to live freely in our midst despite their murder, cursing, blaspheming, lying and defaming." The Counter-Reformation followed suit, using ghettoes to segregate Jews where they lived in Catholic countries and supporting laws which mistreated Jews. Persecution and massacres, particularly in Ukraine and Poland, took place in the seventeenth century. The Enlightenment of the eighteenth century brought about a way of thinking which relied less on superstition and more on rational thought, but the Jews did not benefit from the philosophy. As philosophers of the Enlightenment scorned religion, they blamed Judaism for having been the original source of Christianity and its primitive beliefs; Voltaire was contemptuous of the Jews and their practices.

Ironically, the persecutions built the Jewish community into a unified population with an identity forged by its isolation from the other faiths. Equally ironic is the fact that the bloody French Revolution extended to Jews an opportunity to be regarded as equals in a new society where religion was not the deciding metric. That way of thinking, however, was also destined to fade; Napoleon conquered German states, and the Jews achieved some freedoms, but they did not achieve complete emancipation until Germany was unified in 1871.

As the power of religion over the state ceased to be dominant, nationalism arose in populations and with it, a form of anti-Semitism which held that Jews were inferior to the superior Aryan race. Politicians, now holding sway where formerly clergy had dominated, found it expedient to blame Jews for whatever social or economic woes a country or community was suffering from. By the end of the nineteenth century, Vienna elected a mayor whose anti-Semitic rhetoric inspired an organized political movement. The writings of Mayor Karl Lueger inspired a young Austrian named Adolf Hitler who found much to admire in the anti-Semitic stance of the Viennese mayor.

Chapter Two

Adolf Hitler and the Preservation of the Aryan Race

"Anti-Semitism is exactly the same as delousing. Getting rid of lice is not a question of ideology, it is a matter of cleanliness. In just this same way anti-Semitism for us has not been a question of ideology but a matter of cleanliness."

—Heinrich Himmler

In 1916, a soldier named Adolf Hitler went home on sick leave from the German army. He was dismayed at the low morale and the level of anti-war sentiment that he witnessed among the German population. World War I, which had begun with magnificent, sweeping victory for the German military, had bogged down into trench warfare. No one knew when the war would end, but the German people knew that the sure victory of 1914 was now in doubt. Hitler, who was a lance corporal in the Bavarian army, blamed Jews; it was the Jews, he believed, who had joined forces with the goal of undermining the German war effort.

Hitler's grudge against Jews was also personal. He believed that his mother's death from cancer was the fault of a Jewish doctor. When he applied to the Vienna Academy of Art, his application was rejected because he did not have a certificate that he had left school. His drawings were rejected because they were landscapes and didn't have enough people included in them. He was convinced that a Jewish professor was responsible for rejecting his art school application. He worked removing snow in an area where the wealthy lived, and he believed that Jews lived in the houses. Later when he wrote *Mein Kampf*, he described his time in Vienna as "five years of hardship and misery" and blamed the Jews. He admitted, "I began to hate them."

Hitler, who was Austrian, had moved to Munich in 1913 upon receiving an inheritance from his father's estate. He may have made the move to avoid being drafted into the Austrian army; Hitler's explanation was that he did not want to serve in his country's military because the Austro-Hungarian Empire allowed what he called a mixing of the races in its armed forces.

He received permission to serve in the German army when World War I broke out in August 1914. Hitler was decorated twice for bravery; he was recommended for the Iron Cross First Class by a Jewish lieutenant in his regiment. He was in the hospital after suffering a mustard-gas attack in October 1918 when he learned that the Germans had surrendered to the Allies.

The punishing terms of the Treaty of Versailles instilled in him a desire to bring Germany from defeat to glory again. "When I was confined to bed, the idea came to me that I would liberate Germany, that I would make it great. I knew immediately that it would be realized."

The terms of the treaty ended his ambition to remain in the army, as the German military was disbanded, so he returned to Munich. He fell under the influence of Anton Drexler, the founder of the German Workers' Party (DAP), and joined the Party at Drexler's invitation in 1919. At the time, the DAP only had 40 members, but Hitler recognized that in the Party's anti-Semitic, anti-Communist nationalist philosophy, he had found his political home. The Party changed its name to the National Socialist German Workers Party, but the nickname Nazi was used both by party loyalists and enemies.

The Party had its finger on the pulse of German anger. The Germans were still furious over the terms of the Treaty of Versailles, and the Party supported this view. Germany in the 1920s was rife with right-wing factions who believed that, as Hitler put it, the country had been stabbed in the back. The Nazis published a leaflet blaming 300 international bankers and financiers for their influence over the world economies. "Shake off your Jewish leaders . . . Don't expect anything from the Bolsheviks (the Russian government is nine-tenths Jewish). Bolshevism is a Jewish swindle."

Downtrodden Germans believed that in the Nazi Party, they had found their voice. They joined and used their muscle to disrupt the meetings of other political parties, employing the thuggish violence that would become a trademark. Hitler was the most charismatic of the Nazi Party's leaders, and his speeches mesmerized his audiences. Hitler used his leverage: make him the leader of the Party or he would leave it.

But the Nazi Party didn't have the funds to make itself powerful over all the others, even though circumstances appeared to be in its favor. A financial crisis in 1923 that struck the middle class turned citizens against the government. Hitler felt that if the Nazis could seize Munich and turn it into their power base, they would be able to drive the middle class to action.

On November 8, 1923, he and 2,000 Nazis marched through Munich to take over a meeting at the Munich Beer Hall that was being led by three influential Bavarian politicians. His efforts failed, and he was arrested and tried for treason. He became a national figure as a result, even though he was sent to prison.

Incarceration did not impede Hitler's political career. The guards were friendly. His prison cell looked out on a view of the river. He welcomed guests regularly and was permitted to receive mail from his supporters. He was given a private secretary to help with his correspondence. While in prison, he deduced that in order to bring about his aims, he had to be viewed as a legitimate political leader. During his prison sentence, he wrote *Mein Kampf,* which meant "My Struggle," introducing Hitler to a broader German audience that was receptive to his message of Germany as a superior power. In 1924, he was pardoned by the Bavarian Supreme Court, despite the objections of the state prosecutor, and released from prison.

But things seemed to be improving in Germany. Would Hitler's message still resonate if the country found itself able to prosper and overcome the humiliation of the Treaty of Versailles and the resulting economic hardship that shackled the German people? Thanks to loans from other countries, especially the United States, Germany was beginning to climb out of the morass that the Treaty of Versailles had inflicted upon the nation. Hyperinflation was getting under control. The Ruhr was once again productive as an industrial center. Moderates in politics were beginning to be heard. There were glimmerings of hope that Germany would climb out of its troubled past.

Then the Wall Street economic crash of October 1929 struck. The United States called back the funds that had been loaned to Germany, leaving Germany without money to invest in its economy. Germany was once again in dire financial distress, and this time, the rest of the world was in the same situation and could not loan the country funds.

Blaming the government, the unemployed workers and dissatisfied citizen turned to the Nazi Party. Hitler promised them a glorious Reich that would last a thousand years. Before the financial crisis, the Nazis had only received three percent of the vote in the national elections. When elections were held in July 1932, the Nazis won 40 percent of the vote, making it the largest party in the German Reichstag or Parliament.

Germans who despaired of the future came from all classes, including those who lost their jobs as a result of the economic depression, young people, and others who were members of the lower middle class including small business owners, farmers, office workers, and craftsmen. Hitler's speeches delivered a promise to them that Germany would rise and strike back against its enemies.

The results of the November 1932 elections were less sweeping. The Nazis won 33 percent of the vote, leaving them without a majority. Hitler realized that in order for the Nazis to achieve power, he would need a coalition government. He agreed to join with the conservatives. Negotiations followed, and then President Paul von Hindenberg appointed Hitler as chancellor of the German government.

Chapter Three

The Nazis in Charge

"If the international Jewish financiers in and outside Europe should succeed in plunging the nations once more into a world war, then the result will not be the Bolshevizing of the earth and thus the victory of the Jews, but the annihilation of the Jewish race in Europe!"

—Adolf Hitler

In 1933, Adolf Hitler, the leader of the National Socialist German Workers Party, became chancellor of the German government. The Nazis had only won a plurality of 33 percent of the votes in the 1932 elections, but it was enough. With the victory of the Nazi Party in the German elections, Adolf Hitler was poised to convince the German people that the nation would rise from its degrading defeat in World War I and would see itself as the master of Europe.

The new government cabinet included three members of the Nazi Party: Adolf Hitler, who was appointed chancellor; Wilhelm Frick who was named Minister of the Interior, and Herman Goering, Minister without Portfolio and Prussia's Minister of the Interior. The conservatives felt that they would be able to keep power and maintain control over the Nazis. In general, the world didn't regard Hitler's accession to power as a dire threat. The conservatives failed to realize that Hitler had no intention of serving. He intended to lead. The current crop of politicians had not restored Germany to its destiny; that was Adolf Hitler's crusade. Only he could save Germany.

In order to achieve this goal, it was necessary to purge the country of the forces that could impede him. Dissent could not be tolerated, therefore Hitler took advantage of emergency clauses in the country's constitution which suspended the rights to free speech, assembly, and the press. His security forces, which consisted of the Gestapo, the Storm Troopers or SA, and the SS, arrested or killed members of the opposition parties, including liberals, socialists, and Communists. With the government now devoid of dissenting voices, he was able to pass the Enabling Act of March 23, 1933, which granted Hitler dictatorial powers. The official title of the Enabling Act was Law to Remedy the Distress of People and Reich. For four years, Hitler and his Cabinet could impose laws without the Reichstag's input or approval. In order to make sure that the legislation passed without violating the German Constitution, which needed a two-thirds majority in order to be enacted, the Nazis arrested the Communist members of the government and prevented some of the Social Democrats from attending the session.

Political opponents and trade unionists were arrested and labelled enemies of the state. Homosexuals were sent to concentration camps. Jehovah's Witnesses were banned because their religious beliefs forbade them from swearing an oath to the state or joining the military. Many were sent to prison or concentration camps; their children were sent to orphanages or juvenile detention centers. Others lost their jobs and social welfare benefits such as unemployment and pensions.

Hitler had not forgotten that, in his view, the Jews were to blame for their failure to support the German war effort in World War I. He felt that he must make sure that they were powerless to do this a second time. In order to do so, he believed, the real enemy of Germany had to be eradicated. The census of 1933 counted approximately half a million Jews living in Germany. Under Hitler, that number would be drastically and systematically reduced.

Nazi Propaganda Minister Joseph Goebbels was adept at using available media to promote anti-Semitism as a national moral cause. Hitler was convinced that Jews were engaged in an international conspiracy with the goal of achieving world domination. Hitler and the Nazis did not intend to allow the Jews to undermine this Aryan crusade which would mark Germany's rightful place as the leader of the European nations. He blamed them for the way in which Germany had lost its fighting spirit in World War I and for the devastating economic depression which had crippled the country. The same would not happen in the next war. For of course, there would be another war, so that Germany could gain territory and assert its dominance over Europe. But this time, Germany would win, Hitler promised the people. First, however, Germany must conquer the enemies within.

The Nazis addressed this issue with legislation. Jews were forced to register. Jews were not allowed to work in universities, the courts, or civil service. The Nuremberg Laws, which defined Jews according to the religious affiliation of their grandparents, were passed in April 1933. Laws passed a few years later continued to diminish the freedom of the Jews. Jews were segregated; they could not attend public school or go to the theatre or the movies. They could not visit resorts on vacation. There were sections of German cities where they were not allowed to walk. Jewish business owners were either forced to sell their businesses at absurdly low prices or the businesses and property were seized.

In the Nazi view of ethnicity, the Germans were racially superior, a master race. The disabled, the Jews, Gypsies and other ethnic groups were inferior and were a threat to the purity of the Aryan race. Nazi scientists supported this view and endorsed the notion of eugenics, or selective breeding, in order to maintain the purity of the master race. Between 1933 and 1935, forced sterilization programs were carried out on more than 300,000 people who were physically or mentally disabled so that they would not be able to reproduce. The reasoning for doing this was, the Nazis said, to relieve communities of the financial burden of caring for the handicapped. The Gypsies, who numbered around 30,000, were forcibly sterilized. Blacks and Gypsies or Romani were forbidden to intermarry with Germans.

Legislation was one way of addressing what Hitler regarded as the Jewish problem. Violence was another. On

November 1938, the Nazis attacked German and Austrian Jews on what would become known as the Night of Broken Glass or Kristallnacht. Synagogues and Jewish businesses were destroyed and Jewish men were arrested. Homes were vandalized and innocent people were murdered. Approximately 30,000 Jewish men were sent to concentration camps; a few hundred Jewish women were sent to jails.

It was a warning of what was to come and some heeded it. Germany was home to just over 500,000 Jews. Nearly half of the German-Jewish population and more than two-thirds of Austrian Jews left Germany for other parts of Europe, the United States, and Palestine, Latin America, and Shanghai, which was occupied by the Japanese but did not require a visa to enter. The rest, either because they did not want to leave their home or because they lacked the funds to leave or could not obtain visas or sponsors in other countries, remained in Germany. It was their death sentence.

Chapter Four

The Final Solution to the Jewish Question

"The Führer has ordered the Final Solution of the Jewish question. We, the SS, have to carry out this order. I have therefore chosen Auschwitz for this purpose."

— Rudolf Höss

Hitler decided that the goals of war were not merely to achieve *lebensraum* or living space for the German people. The Reichstag was going to global war to rid the world of the Jewish menace which occupied Europe and Russia. SS Obergrubbenfuhrer Reinhard Heydrich agreed that in order to accomplish this feat, Europe would "be combed through from west to east." According to Heydrich, there were 11 million Jews living in Europe and Russia. Those Jews could be sent to Poland, where the SS had organized ghettoes to contain the population. Food rations at starvation level were one means of accomplishing the grotesque Nazi goal of eliminating the Jewish people.

A young woman who lived in the Lodz ghetto described the effects of hunger: "Slowly, slowly the Germans were achieving their goal. I think they let us suffer from hunger, not because there was not enough food, but because this was their method of demoralizing us, of degrading us, of torturing us. These were their methods, and they implemented these methods scrupulously. Therefore we had very many, many deaths daily. Very many sick people for whom there was no medication, no help, no remedy. We just stayed there, and lay there, and the end was coming."

But for the Nazis, the ghettoes were not fast enough. In southeast Poland, at Belzec, Treblinka, and Sobibor, the Germans built gas chambers with crematories and burial pits nearby. In Upper Silesia nearby, the building ensued on a grander scale as Auschwitz was constructed. Every Jew must be killed, Hitler ordained. It didn't matter whether they had contributed to society; they were not worthy to live. Auschwitz would be the final destination of Jews, Gypsies, political opponents such as Communist, and the mentally and physically handicapped. They were not pure and in Hitler's perspective, their presence was a contaminant. Auschwitz was located on a former military base near Krakow, Poland. Factories that had been in the area were appropriated; people who lived in the area where forced to leave their homes so that the structures could be razed.

Auschwitz was chosen to be an extermination camp rather than a concentration camp because it was close to the center of the countries which were occupied by the Nazis. It was also situated near the rail lines that would be used to transport those who were taken from their homes. The camp, with its barbed wire fencing and 28 watch towers patrolled by armed guards, was inescapable.

Auschwitz was also a labor camp where the detainees were used to produce synthetic rubber, munitions, and products needed for the German war effort. Auschwitz I contained more than 15,000 political prisoners. Auschwitz II, which was located in Birkenau, was built in 1941 and was large enough to hold 90,000. In Auschwitz II were the bathhouses and Crematoria II, III, IV, and V where those who were to be exterminated were sent. It was here, at Birkenau, where most of the prisoners died. The proximity of the barracks to the gas chambers was not happenstance. The smell of burned flesh and hair could be detected by the people in the barracks, reminding them that they too could end up gassed.

The Nazis had begun building concentration camps in 1933 after they rose to power in Germany. Originally, the camps held approximately 45,000 political opponents and union organizers who were deemed enemies of the state in Hitler's view. In 1934, Heinrich Himmler, leader of the SS, was in charge of all the camps in Germany and under his authority, the population of the camps expanded to hold those regarded as racially undesirable. The concentration camps did not have the same scope as the extermination camps which utilized gas chambers to murder Jews en masse. The first such camp to open was Dachau, which was founded in 1933 for Communists and German politicians who opposed Hitler.

In 1940, Auschwitz-Birkenau, the largest of the German camps, opened in southern Poland. Originally, it was used as a detention center for political prisoners; before long, the network of camps assumed the purpose for which it would become notorious, and it didn't take long before it became the center where people who were regarded as undesirable and expendable by the Nazi state were sent to the gas chambers.

Trains arrived several times a day from the German-occupied countries with a Jewish population, each train carrying more than one thousand people bound for the death camps. There was no room on the trains to sit down, they were given nothing to eat, and if they needed to use the toilet, buckets had to suffice. The people imprisoned inside the trains didn't know where they were going or what their fate was. The journey could last as long as ten days and many of the people on board died of hunger, suffocation, or illness.

Upon arrival at Auschwitz, the trains emptied their prisoners onto a ramp alongside the railway line. When the trains pulled up to the unloading ramp, the SS guards, kapos, and the Sonderkommando were waiting. Other inmates of the camp were assigned the task of getting the new arrivals out of the train cars. The prisoners were forced out of the train cars, leaving the possessions they had brought with them behind.

They lined up for the selection process, the men in one line, the women in the other; more than 80 percent of those who arrived were immediately sent to their death. German SS soldiers, armed with whips and attack dogs, marched up and down the platforms. Those who were selected to live would face inhumane treatment working as slave labor. One young woman, Edith Birkin, who was taken to Auschwitz, recalled that she made sure to look strong and healthy so that she would not be sent with the elderly and the sick. "If you were old or ill-looking, you went to the other side. From what I remember," she later recorded, "I never met anybody over thirty after [the arrival]."

When the detainees—most of them Jews by the middle of 1942—arrived at Auschwitz, they were examined by the staff of Nazi doctors, which numbered around 30. If they were young children or elderly people, pregnant or ill, they were sent to what they believed were showers. But instead of water for showering, the prisoners were exposed to Zyklon-B, a poisonous gas, which killed them. Their bodies were sent to the crematoria.

Those who were capable of working escaped the gas chambers for the time being, but the work was grueling, the conditions debilitating; food was insufficient and nutrition nonexistent; living conditions were terrible. Daily life included executions, torture, and the demeaning struggle to survive.

Chapter Five

The Angel of Death

"There can't be two smart peoples in the world. We're going to win the war, so only the Aryan race will stand."

—Josef Mengele

He was not the only physician assigned to Auschwitz. He wasn't even the highest-ranking physician in the camp. But it is Dr. Josef Mengele whose medical malevolence looms largest over the legacy of Auschwitz. Known as the Angel of Death or the White Angel, Mengele accompanied the 30 physicians who made their rounds in the camp, determining which arrivals could work and which would be sent immediately to the gas chambers. He was known for appearing fastidiously dressed in his Nazi uniform, even when he wasn't on duty, when the arrivals came to the camp so that he could take part in the process of deciding who would live and who would die.

Mengele, who was born in 1911, studied physical anthropology and medicine at the University of Munich, receiving a PhD. In 1937, he went to work at the Institute for Hereditary Biology and Racial Hygiene, joining Dr. Otmar von Verschuer, whose research focused on twins. That same year, Mengele joined the Nazi Party and the following year, the Schutzstaffel or SS. Drafted into the

German army in 1940, he served in a medical capacity until he was wounded. Returning to Germany in 1943, he once again joined Dr. von Verschuer at the Kaiser Wilhelm Institute for Anthropology, Human Genetics and Eugenics.

In May of that year, Captain Mengele was transferred to Auschwitz. He made a memorable impression in the selection process as he determined which new arrivals would live and which would die. Survivors reported that to be sent to the left meant death; directed to the right was life. Usually, children under the age of 15 were sent to the chambers, but one 13-year-old girl, Ann Feng Fosenheck, was allowed to live; her mother, sister, and her sister's children were sent to their death by Mengele. "They went straight into the gas chamber. I on the other hand was brought into a barrack."

For Mengele, Auschwitz was a laboratory where there were no constraints and he was free to explore his research under any terms he chose. Twins were regarded as a means of studying the way in which heredity and environment affected a person's health. When he was working at legitimate research facilities, Mengele had conducted authentic experiments with twins as test subjects. But at Auschwitz, he was able to experiment in a manner which allowed him free rein to conduct whatever sort of research, with whatever ramifications, he chose. In a camp occupied by Jewish and Romani test subjects, Mengele's murderous exploration into the fields of his interest was nothing short of barbarous. If a subject died as a result of his experiments, there were no repercussions. They were all under a death sentence anyway. He considered himself a scientist, keeping records and noting the height, weight, and comparisons of the twins as if he was legitimately researching them—but science did not embrace pain with the zeal that Mengele displayed.

He operated on some twins without using anesthesia, removing limbs or genitals. He killed others so that he could dissect them and preserve body parts. If one of the twins died as a result of the experimental operation, the other was sent to the gas chamber, no longer of use since comparisons were no longer possible.

One survivor recalled Mengele's experiment with Siamese twins. Two children were taken from the camp; one of the children was hunchbacked. Several days later, the children were returned. The hunchbacked child had been sewn to the other child, back to back; their wrists were sewn back to back as well. Gangrene had set in and the witness recalled that the children cried every night before they died soon after.

Mengele, devoted to a distorted and sadistic version of science, was convinced that by harvesting tissue samples and body parts of Jews and Gypsies, he would be able to scientifically prove that the race had degenerated and was inferior to German blood. He was attempting to provide evidence that this inferiority made these ethnic groups more susceptible to certain diseases. At Auschwitz, there was no fallout when his human experiments died as a result of his testing; in fact, Mengele was free to have them murdered so that he could do post-mortems on them.

One of his areas of interest, in addition to twins, was heterochromia, which referred to a condition of someone whose irises were two different colors. Part of his research included collecting the eyes of the people who died from his experiments in order to provide research material for a colleague who was studying eye pigmentation. A Jewish prisoner recalled that at the Gypsy camp, there was a wooden table. On the table were eyes of different colors, including pale yellow, bright blue, green, and violet. Each sample was labelled and numbered.

Another survivor recalled an episode when a large number of the SS, including Mengele, came to the camp on motorcycles and gathered around a fire that had been started. Ten trucks arrived soon after. The trucks, filled with children, were backed up to the fire and the guards began to throw the children from the dump trucks into the fire. The children screamed and some tried to escape, but if they were able to crawl out of the flames, one of the SS would push the child back in.

Mengele also conducted research on a form of gangrene which destroyed the mucous membrane of the mouth and tissues, using camp inmates who suffered from the condition for his documentation.

His aims were to promote his professional advancement, and he hoped that he would be able to use his research to present a second postdoctoral dissertation as part of the admission process to a university where he hoped to become a professor. During the 21 months that Mengele spent at Auschwitz, he sent an estimated 400,000 prisoners to the gas chambers. Even allowing for the times when he was unable to work due to illness (he suffered from bouts of malaria and typhus), it's estimated that he was responsible for 20,000 deaths per month.

Mengele regarded himself as a scientist; the Auschwitz inmates who were the objects of his experiments meant no more to him that the laboratory rats used in modern-day research. His research papers ended up in the hands of the Allies; they were never published and his experiment results are said to be held in a vault in Israel.

Chapter Six

Life in Auschwitz

"His face remains in my memory to this day. He looked at us as one would a pack of leprous dogs clinging to life. 'Remember it always, let it be graven in your memories. You are in Auschwitz. And Auschwitz is not a convalescent home. It is a concentration camp. Here, you must work. If you don't, you will go straight to the chimney. Work or crematorium—the choice is yours.'"

—Elie Wiesel

The family of Otto Frank had managed to hide from the Nazis for two years, but in 1944, they were arrested by the Nazis and were on their way to Auschwitz. The journey by train took three days. The prisoners were crammed into the train cars, forced to stand because of the crowding. There was a bucket that served as a toilet; the stench soon became unbearable. One passenger recalled that if "by chance, you landed next to an air hole, you had some relief from the stench, but you could catch a cold because it was so drafty."

The trip was exhausting under such conditions. Compared to some of the deportations, which could take as long as ten days, the three-day journey seemed easier in comparison, but the conditions were exhausting and people often died of suffocation or illness. The train carrying the Franks arrived at Auschwitz at 2:00 am. When the doors of the car opened, men in striped uniforms boarded, yelling at the passengers to hurry and get out.

Leaving their possessions behind, the passengers got off the trains as SS soldiers marched up and down the platform, holding whips in their hands, dogs at their sides. Overhead, spotlights shone down upon the scene. The men were told to line up on one side and women on the other. The doctors who examined the arrivals sent the sick, the elderly, and the children to the gas chambers. The others were sent to the barracks. Otto Frank never saw his wife or children again.

That scene was replayed constantly among families who were sent to the camps. The fate of those who were under the illusion that they were sent to the showers was immediate; the showers were gas chambers and they would die. But those who were sent to the barracks were subjected to inhumane treatment that depleted them of strength and health and sometimes even the will to live. Upon entering the camp, the prisoners saw the sign overhead that proclaimed "Work will give you freedom." If any of the new arrivals believed that by working hard, they would be released, they soon learned otherwise. They were slaves in a Nazi extermination camp.

Prisoners who would be assigned to work were tattooed with numbers on their arms. One Holocaust survivor recalled being told, "From now on you do not answer by your name. Your name is your number." The hair on their heads, and pubic hair as well, was shaved. The purpose of this was twofold; in part, it was to combat the problem of lice which was rampant in the camps. It was also done to remove traces of individuality from the prisoners and to degrade them. They were then disinfected, deloused and given the striped cotton uniforms and shoes which were all the same size.

In a bizarre way, life in Auschwitz took on the form of a daily routine. Awakened before dawn, the inmates had to make their beds, which consisted of a thin blanket and a mattress of wooden boards. Punishment was severe if the SS guard was not satisfied with the manner in which the beds was made. The inmates then stood for roll call, sometimes for four hours regardless of the weather, in insufficient clothing which offered no protection from rain or snow, as the guards read the names of the prisoners. The striped uniforms that they were issued upon arrival at the camp were not made of material designed to withstand harsh weather, and the clothing was not changed for months at a time. Roll call itself could lead to death, as the weakest and sickest of the inmates would die as their names were called.

If a prisoner had been caught misbehaving, a penal roll call was conducted. The prisoners were forced to stand through the night, cold, hungry, and weak, as the roll call went on, sometimes accompanied by physical abuse and even shootings.

Breakfast rations were handed out after roll call ended. They were given enough food to keep them alive so that they could work: ten ounces of bread, a small piece of salami or an ounce of margarine, and brown coffee with no sugar or cream.

When breakfast concluded, the second roll call got underway. The inmates were combined into work groups; armed SS guards and attack dogs accompanied them as they went to their work site.

"Canada" was a work site where the possessions taken from the newest arrivals to the camp were sorted. It was known as Canada because of the country's nickname, "the land of plenty." The work site was an open compound with numerous sheds and covered areas. The inmates had scissors so that they could cut open the coat linings to see if the arrivals had tried to hide anything that would be of use to the Nazis. This was a plum job, but it took its toll on those working there because, as they went through belongings and photographs, they realized that families came to an end at Auschwitz.

At noon, the prisoners ate lunch, which was a quart of water with a few vegetables. They then returned to work until dusk fell, when they were led back to the camp for the evening roll call, which took four hours, an arduous ordeal for people who had worked for twelve hours with minimal nourishment. Their supper was bread with rotten salami or margarine and jam and, occasionally, a piece of skim cheese, also rotten.

Toilet facilities were limited and the inmates were allowed a mere ten seconds. They were monitored when they needed to use the toilets. When they went to their barracks for the night, they had to lay sideways in order to fit on the beds, which were occupied by multiple people. It was not uncommon for a person to die during the night.

The beds were infested, and bedbugs were a particular ordeal to be endured, along with lice and rats. The inmates slept on top of the few possessions that they owned, such as a cap or a bowl, so that they wouldn't be stolen by other inmates.

The camp had offices, kitchens, living quarters, and a sick ward that was staffed by physicians who had been sentenced. Anyone who was very ill would not be treated in the sick ward but would be sent to die. The doctors did what they could to conceal illness.

There were three sick wards. They were equipped with one stove for heating. Flooding was a common problem. Beds had no mattresses, and those in the maternity ward were occupied by as many as four women per bed.

A single day would see as many as 1,200 people in the ward; approximately 12 died daily. There were no antiseptics, and women in labor could only be given aspirin for the pain. But the women in the wards showed a remarkable compassion for the children. They would sometimes sacrifice meals in order to gain credit to purchase fabric that could be used to make diapers and clothing for the babies.

The Nazis, however, were not concerned about the health and wellbeing of infants; if they were a bother, they would be killed. Until the summer of 1943, newborn infants were immediately drowned. After that, the Nazis took any children who were born with blonde hair and blue eyes and sent them to live with Nazi families. Hoping that the children would one day be reunited with their birth mother, a Polish midwife who worked in the maternity ward marked the infants with an improvised tattoo. The midwife, named Stanislawa Leszczynska, had been arrested in 1943; her two sons were sent to the stone quarries, and she and her daughter were sent to Auschwitz.

During her years in the camp, Leszczynska was a midwife for the delivery of over 3,000 babies. Delivering live babies in such forbidding conditions was an amazing feat. She had been instructed to kill the children that she delivered and to report them as stillborn, but this she refused to do, although the guards threatened to kill her for her defiance.

The task of delivering babies was subsequently assigned to someone else at the camp, and Leszczynska was ordered to report on her mortality statistics. The officials were dubious that she had not lost a mother or a child during delivery, something that even qualified hospitals in well-equipped German hospitals could not claim.

Another inmate with a medical background, Dr. Miklos Nyiszli, was forced to help Dr. Josef Menele with his experiments in the camp. His duties included performing the autopsies on the dead inmates who were killed as a result of Mengele's experiments. Dr. Nyiszli, who survived the camp, revealed the horror of Auschwitz after the camp was liberated when he returned to his native Hungary and published *Auschwitz: A Doctor's Eyewitness Account.*

Chapter Seven

Liberation and Judgment

"If the day should ever come when we must go, if some day we are compelled to leave the scene of history, we will slam the door so hard that the universe will shake and mankind will stand back in stupefaction."

—Joseph Goebbels

Toward the end of the war, the Soviets were approaching Auschwitz, and the Germans were in a hurry to remove the evidence of their Final Solution. The last roll call at Auschwitz listed 67,012 prisoners. In January 1945, the Germans led 60,000 detainees on a death march to Polish towns 30 miles from Krakow. An estimated 15,000 died on the way, but those who survived the journey were put on trains and taken to concentration camps back in Germany. Anne Frank and her sister were among the first ones to leave Auschwitz. They were sent to Bergen-Belsen where they died of typhus.

Otto Frank recalled that the prisoners were offered a choice of remaining in the camp until the Russian army arrived or traveling 50-kilometers through heavy snow to the border where they would be taken by train to Germany. He chose to stay in the camp. Elie Wiesel chose to march out of the camp. "The choice was in our hands.

For once we could decide our fate for ourselves. We could ... stay ... Or else we could follow the others." Wiesel and his father chose to evacuate.

On January 27, 1945, the Soviets arrived at Auschwitz and found more than 7,000 prisoners who had been left behind. They also found the piles of dead bodies. There were other ghastly mementoes left behind: seven tons of human hair that had been shaved off the heads of those sent to the camp; there were hundreds of thousands of clothing items and shoes. The Russian soldiers discovered that the Germans had attempted to conceal evidence of their extermination policies; the four gas chambers were in ruins. The crematorium ovens had already been dismantled and moved from the camp in November of the previous year. Before abandoning the camp, the Nazis had burned camp records and set fire to the clothing warehouse and some of the barracks.

Inmates of camps that had been liberated by the British and American forces were given care and assistance, but the inmates of Auschwitz were on their own. Prisoners from 29 different countries had to fend for themselves as they made their way back to their homes, encountering hostility as they journeyed from the citizens. One of the survivors who journeyed back home said the Russians didn't liberate them. "We just ran away without permission. No joyous celebration. I never heard the word liberation back then. I didn't even know there was such a word."

Dr. Josef Mengele left the camp on January 17, avoiding the advancing Soviet army by traveling in the guise of a Wehrmacht officer. He left his medical records with a nurse at the Gross-Rosen concentration camp in Lower Silesia. He and members of his unit were captured by the American forces, but because he wasn't on the list of war criminals, he was released and given papers using the false name of Fritz Ullman. He spent several months in flight, working as a farmhand, fearing that if he were captured, he would be tried as a war criminal.

In April, 1949, Mengele escaped from Germany and travelled to Genoa with a false passport he'd obtained from the International Committee of the Red Cross. In July, he sailed to Argentina. In 1956, he was given a foreign residence permit using his real name, Josef Mengele. The Israeli Mossad sought to find him and bring him to justice, and West Germany offered a reward for his capture. Mengele continued to elude his pursuers, fleeing to Paraguay and Brazil. In 1979, he suffered a stroke while he was swimming and drowned.

Stanislawa Lesczynska returned to Poland after the liberation of the camp and continued to work as a midwife. Her children would pursue medical careers and all would become physicians. Hospitals were named after her and the main road to the museum at Auschwitz is named for her. She died in 1974.

When the Soviet army was just a day away, Hitler, who had been sequestered in his underground bunker since January, decided to take his life rather than face the retribution of the Russians. He swallowed a cyanide capsule and shot himself with a pistol. His body and that of Eva Braun, the mistress he married two days before their suicide, were cremated in the garden of the chancellery by others in the bunker. He was not officially declared dead until 1956.

Hitler and Mengele were able to avoid justice. Josef Goebbels and Heinrich Himmler also committed suicide. Had Hitler, Goebbels, and Himmler lived and Mengele remained in captivity, they would have been tried for war crimes. Between 1945 and 1949, thirteen trials were held in Nuremberg, Germany. Winston Churchill had favored summary execution without trials, but the Americans wanted legal proceedings so that documentation could be presented to avoid any protestations that the defendants had been unjustly accused.

There was no precedent for an international war crimes trial and Great Britain, France, the Soviet Union, and the United States needed to establish a uniform process for the trials to proceed. Nuremberg was chosen as the site for the trials because its Palace of Justice had a large prison area that had not been greatly damaged during the war. Another reason to hold the trials in Nuremberg was because the city had been the location of the massive rallies by the Nazis.

Twelve of those on trial were sentenced to death, one in absentia. The remaining defendants were sentenced to prison; their terms ranged from ten years to life. Herman Goering, who had hidden a cyanide capsule in a jar of skin medication, committed suicide the night before he was to be executed.

Trials were also conducted to hear the case against the doctors who conducted their medical experiments upon the inmates; German industrialists who had used slave labor were tried as well. Not everyone was executed for their crimes. But as a result of the Nuremberg Trials, the United Nations Genocide Convention and the Geneva Convention on the Laws and Customs of War were formed.

Nuremberg did not bring a halt to the practice of genocide in the post-war world, which continues to enact what is called ethnic cleansing against a segment of the population. But Nuremberg did establish the perspective that crimes against humanity would be tried in an international court.

Today, the Auschwitz-Birkenau Memorial and Museum in Oswiecim, Poland, honors the memory of the victims of Nazi persecution. In 1947, the museum was founded with the decree that it was to be kept forever as a monument to the martyrdom of Poland and the other nations who suffered from Nazi atrocities. The World Cultural Heritage took ownership of the former concentration camp in 1979 and since that time, more than 25 million visitors have toured the museum. In 1979, Polish-born Pope John Paul II held a mass in Birkenau. The Pope recognized the horror of the Holocaust, and he also acknowledged that the rest of the world, including the Roman Catholic Church, had not done enough to prevent the murder of the Jews. In 1998, the Vatican formally apologized for its inaction. Pope John Paul II labelled the camp "Golgotha of our times," referring to the site where Jesus Christ was crucified.

Nuremberg could try the perpetrators of the Holocaust, but there is no way to sentence those who hate. Anti-Semitism continues to summon prejudice toward people who have committed no crime but who are judged as inferior by those who prefer to hate. There has been a resurgence in hate crimes as members of nationalistic factions preach their venomous messages. Political parties have won seats in their legislative bodies because their violent messages have found a willing audience.

As long as hatred and prejudice are sown in the hearts and minds of people who refuse to acknowledge that human beings are all more alike than unalike, the shadow of Auschwitz will continue to fall over civilization.

Printed in Great Britain
by Amazon